Noelle Kocot

Humanity

SurVision Books

First published in 2018 by
SurVision Books
Dublin, Ireland
www.survisionmagazine.com

Copyright © Noelle Kocot, 2018

Design © SurVision Books, 2018

ISBN: 978-1-9995903-0-7

This book is in copyright. No part of this publication may be reproduced, stored in a retrieval system or transmitted in any form or by any means without the prior permission in writing from the publisher.

For Monica Antolik, Stephanie Horn and Daniel Kramoris

Acknowledgements

Grateful acknowledgement is made to the editors of the following, in which a number of these poems originally appeared:
"The Moon", "The Revolution", "Tribute", "Courtyard Poem", "Tongues", "Poem for my 48th Year": *SurVision Poetry Magazine.*

CONTENTS

The Moon 4
The Revolution 5
Tribute 6
Courtyard Poem 7
Tongues 8
Poem for my 48th Year 9
Non-Judgment 10
March 12th, 2018 11
The Lathe 12
The Terrarium 13
Quality of Life 14
The St. Paddy's Day Party 15
Letter to Paul 10/17/17 16
Winter's Grace 17
"I Want All My Garmonbozia" 18
Starting from Scratch 19
Elegy of Lazarus 20
Clarity of the Spheres 21
On Unselfishness 22
Maundy Thursday 23
March for Our Lives 24
After a Blowout 25
The Dish 26
Small 27
A Triumph of Love 28
The Freedom 29
On Surgery 30
Humanity 31
A Century 32

The Moon

Elsewhere, the music moves. Did you
Find this road with depth and splash,
Oh from our beds, we must not immolate
Ourselves. The other look you bought,

Time free of hazard, the tower leans into
The rain. We shut the hours as clouds
Surround our heads. A hint of spring
Slides over the sill, as young as time in

The gray February marshes. I have something
To give you, no? And the vines covering
A disgrace amid the maples. A thaw of
What wet sky surrounds, the cries over all

The alarms, our gardens filled with weeds,
The offhand way in which you plunge
In the aproned dusk, what surrounds the
Worms as the moon comes out, their schemes.

The Revolution

Your dishonesty is matched only by your
Love. We must choose our alliances carefully.
Or indeed, the gothic scraps of wind
Against the dawn, our words filling like

Sails. Racing past the courtyard, our aprons
Hemmed, the schemes and tasks of the day
Are like a little home. As you lie beneath
A quilt, you travel twice to see the eclipse.

God makes the village green. So we shall
Be severed, and the night knows of supreme
Loss. Tranquil and bright, I find life waking
Like a menacing cloud, but strewn with half

Notes underneath the fold. Lightning held
To a visible alphabet, you say something, while I hold the
                                                              view.

Tribute

The tyrannical rocks, a bridge unrented.
Where should I go with my gleaming lipstick,
A town hushed and no rush of wind. I have
Gone past indifference into passion with one

Flick of a channel. It took impossibly long,
With me being only half alive in the glimmer of
Him and what he saw. Now, with the glaze
Over the world as it is, now with the veins

Of sunlight crashing over these costumes,
We are pulled down deep into the freezing
Waters, we are welcomed by an ugliness so
Alien. It is night now, and the people come in

From the streets. I stand beholden to the beaches,
Where the authoritarian waves wash out to sea.

Courtyard Poem

Porch dawn, the roots of shapes
Made mutual. There's no one to
Point east anymore. What cannot
Be separated, what gives itself
Completely to perception, the gray
Muck that follows heat, and when
The time comes to leave we can
Say we have named a whole identity.
Give me that dense key without
Incident. A bus has picked me up
And left me off blind. The breast
Is a decision, oh mon cher, I give you
A live tree with its music twisting,
Then I think you were torn away.

Tongues

A genus of brown, like bird teeth,
Like a tiny array of helplessnesses.
Time is a shape. Time is a shape.
Too menacing to mention, I have
Shut all the doors, and yet. A hypothetical
Quarter makes us pause. I understand
These words, child, sun, pen,
And I don't know where the ladder
Is denied. It is the absence of scene,
The fruit rabid and going to waste.
If I speak in tongues, it's so you'll understand.

Poem for my 48th Year

Watch it dissolve, this earth that blooms.
I can remember the words to that song,
I can take up "space" like a version of the
Same field we walked on, in the crush
Of weeds. I give you back your energy,
And I take mine, and now the design
Has been completed. What else can I
Do but write these clean lines, lit from
Without. No argument, these roses
Most articulated in this town, the light
Streaming like a bastard with a chemical
Snow as each minute collapses. Live
Sparks that acclimate to this new weather,
The human sunlight like the varnish on a hand.

Non-Judgment

Balance indeed on this hurricane. Shadows
Came in the thunder. I touched your sleeve,
The actions gone, disappeared. Spring's
Blue day and the nightfall fog. I wear his ring

Still, and I am standing around waiting like
The egg the chicken bears. Titular throne,
A permanent solution, experiments on a balcony.
I see bad things arising, but if I live spackled

With dust, I will drop like a black strap from
A Coach bag over all of New Jersey. Careless
And deep, if you wish, I will send you a single
Note of music. Where is my white pen that

Writes in milk? The stars are merely moments.
The slipshod consonants, the vowels like laughter
In your wreath. Point me in that direction, then
Shut your eyes across the chambers, a waltz of hours.

March 12th, 2018

Somehow you knew it would be an
Epic, the cricket music in June, the
Warm bath towels on the ascendant
Hour. One string of thunder, and then

Nothing, no more hell, no more dying.
Then porridge in another dubious station.
We got off somewhere in Arles, and the
Understanding of those forests never

Left. I waved to you. You were not
Imperial. You said something, a fact
That I longed to hear, and I saw his
Beautiful face tangled in the trees. If

I write poetry, if I write poetry, then
Maybe this voyage will be caught in its
Own weight of the difficulties strung
Around my neck like tiny shells. Another

Boatman's dust, what was fed on an
Obedient portion of this view, died simply
Again, and then opens all the courtyards.
The rhapsody of my longings cry tears of lye.

The Lathe

Evanescence to make a visible alphabet,
Without which, I am drowning. Slow
Murmur In a cave of apples, how we treat
The sand with our feet—like a tiny home.

Don't be afraid. That sculpture in summer
Is like a mysterious plant. I'm tired. No,
I'm lying. I have so much energy and desire
And enough greenery that I don't wither

Away. It's like vespers in New Jersey, we
Sing "around" them rather than sparsely.
Chewing the despised gum, I give you one
Piece and all is dancing on its head. Now,

Splashing the waves, now we wake up and
Repeat, the cords of the rivers run around
Again, and we begin to relax. I never meant
That it was only here, the drama, the lathe.

The Terrarium

Vivid terrarium, I have more trouble
Finding you than what belongs to memory
& actors. Day lightens into afternoon,
The tortoises walk around so peacefully,

And you, my aching comet are the sleeve
Of my dreams. We are fortified by the
Moment. Our outer garments held tight
Across the skies like pandemonium. I

Said once, this dark meter in the dissolving
Spring means nothing anymore. Hand over
Fist, we are "building" something in another
Country. If I surrender to the lull and hum

Of so much rain, if I fall like a comma, gobbling
Up the dirt, I will meet you on the shoreline,
Tucked and waiting as a lone sock in a ladle
Made for our various sauces. Super blue to you!

Quality of Life

Conjuring plunging arrows, the
Fragments of an island surround me.
Sun rises, sun sets. Over a bay window
I saw the smile to an introduction

Between us from long ago. How many
Hours have I wasted today? One tree
Later, I gather up my things. How can
I explain Matisse? The transparent

Toughness of a moment, neighbors
Who admire each other, my floral dress
Tucked beneath my legs. Have some
Coke. The uncle who yells at you through

His moustache is now vacationing in
Germany. In what way should I "describe"
Him? We are in the village now, and
The blooming of vowels in the evening goes dark.

The St. Paddy's Day Party

Covetousness in the kitchen, elsewhere,
The music moves us. Who says this breath
Of wind aligns us with the margins? I have
Lost it all, but found myself at this party,

This innocuous hypothesis where the adults
Running in syllables over the grass watch
Their hips. Flowers on the walls, green candy
On the tables. Who has escaped virtue?

Who is wild? The chairs shelter us from ourselves,
And the 90 year old chemist shows me her
Cross, soldered onto her late husband's cross.
I am through with everything, but at the same

Time, there is fruit at home, a chill of waiting,
And the night's fog seems less important. Let
Us lie our heads in the sun. Let us stroll like
Odalisques in the depth and splash of history.

Letter to Paul 10/17/17

Meditating is all good, but everything
Is Zazen. We perceive what exists. In
The last place is love, which howls like
A wounded animal, the supposed lightness

While you wait in dangerous time. His
Hair contrasts with his godliness. Photo-
Like presence, the golden lilies with known,
Unmediating symptoms. Winter squalls.

The leaf detaches from the tree, and I
Think of you over the pasturing. Blandishment
Of a solitary cry in the evening. Trakl knew
It best, drunk, ill. The moonlight dares to

Remember, like saying, this is possible,
And the love comes back like pliancy.

Winter's Grace

Morning's warm cheek, a plan of
The stratosphere. Glazed, we go
Upward, into an exhalation of smoke
And being human. Quick! See what
You've laved and extended. Joy
In the fugue, the branching of an echo.
My brothers, you are all vim and vigor
And you are active in a blank wall
Of silence. What is consumed is the
Summer remembrance of an aspect
Of the stars, flung out like an orchestra
And dyed like a memory of the cold.

"I Want All My Garmonbozia"

The spell now over, recast In some other
Light. Dark avenues of cold jinx the shadows.
What were you holding in the budding
Trees? The idea of heaven is an island somewhere—

You'll never reach it in this life. The rain
Descends into a marsh, and where are you?
"You" are firmly planted in reality. You
Are so much disenchantment on the unreadable

Ink of the dawn-light. What is the speed of
This river? Poet laureate, I could go on like
This, through the current of my life's subject.
You are linked to the essence of this very house,

And the fish fry is tonight. What air have you
Almost breathed, what channels of thought
Have you spoken? An overblown alphabet
That awaits is where home is. Only thickening fog.

Starting from Scratch

This road is breathless. But we stop
Sometimes, and we feel the indifference
Coming on us like a giant canvas, on
Which flowers are painted. The rain

Of us chalks the body. If nothing, I keep
Breathing, dangerously close to the
City's long paradigm. If you have grown
Accustomed to the twists of the wind,

If you have seen these papers flying
Overhead like giant moths, then I will
Show you the ineradicable bleeding of
The print, where we publish ourselves.

Suppose you weren't watching for a
Moment. Suppose whatever you've made
Is evidence of someone's being here.
If I offend you, I may be wrong to charm the gift.

Elegy of Lazarus

Softening the sun, what was that
Fog-haunted shell? Twice begotten,
My "communication" is ripe and ready.
Oh, go your way with your animal

Around your neck, unseen is the neck
Of heaven on the horizon. If you plant
Your distinct doorway too far over,
Then something develops like the kill

Instincts in his sippy cup. A clumsy
Line, the curve of her young waist,
I am strangled by a wilderness of thought,
And I don't know where I end anymore.

But I have seen the fierceness forged
In memory, I have given a geography
To the vegetables I serve. There,
The subject lies sleeping, then struts forth.

Clarity of the Spheres

I took my place among the elements,
Then dark struck again, again. In the
Deep chambers, the old magazine
Cracked open, and there was the dizziness

Of disgrace absconding from the mid-
Morning sky. The creation hides the view,
The mountain covered in sharp lines.
Ominous in the empathic rain, the leaves

Sheeted the sidewalks like a mirror.
A decision has been made. The dimensions
Express a shadow where none exists.
Folds of skin fall from my arms, the tenure

Of tossed sand. Earth tones beleaguer
Their own denuding, weightlessness begins.

On Unselfishness

Jeweled tones, anyone can be excluded
In a room. But that's okay. If I could think
Of anything outside the music, the huge
Glaze of sunrise would be enough. Suspended

As I am before the ending, a glance at all
The junk, the city's bridges hold you like
Butter knives. Who is the cause of you?
Hands cover us until we reach our stop. One

Single bit of news from the outskirts, I can
Tell you now to leave it alone. A tidal flirt
In the waves, a quick song over the Seine,
Before anyone realizes my mistake, I grant

You feathers on the waters. I get you the
Seltzer. This glow on the paper is my reward.

Maundy Thursday

There is something very right about
My life. The blue skies dream, drenched
In mercury, the fog over the city bears
Its roots. When I fall to my knees because

I am hurt, the dozen dimmed chains around
My ankles seem well enough in their place.
A sadness pervades the rooms. I am not
Without wisdom, nor do I take the stage

To tell you about it anymore. This saga
With its intermissions, this bread I give you
Nightly, is just a continuous dimmed curiosity
So permanently revised. I go toward the

Surface of sidewalks in their golden perimeters
And reach up to the gates of yellow and collision.

March for Our Lives

Like a cool and patient animal, like
The pigeon carrying its message, where
Do we find ourselves, here, together,
While the others look on, thick with shame?

You never opened the window, but
You stepped into an unlit space. Fever
Abstracted from its head, the draft of falling,
Falling, it's the cursive for rain, the remote

Figure in a mirror. We can prove that nothing
Comes into being by itself. Through death's
Endless signs, I see that nothing is touching
Me. We have a hard time on that water,

But we stay without our petal coats floating
Therein. I was inconsolable, I met you on
A frieze of daylight, and then went off, a mystical
Human cry in the darkness, hurrying back aloft.

After a Blowout

Fury at the wingtips, it's easy to
Be functional and to dream! I put
Away my childhood in exchange for
Lifelong sadness—nothing ends but

Errs. Configurations collapse—a moonlit
Verb racing across the sea of night. A
Troubled parallel, my home, invaded.
I stand to learn something, but what of

The undulant beginnings slopping their
Ways across a sodden sky? Those who
Make rain die early in springtime. The
Style of what binds and measures what

Words do and do not. A miracle is at
Hand, oh, my sweetness! Letter after
Letter, we exchange the days like crumb
Cakes over the earth's silver passages.

The Dish

Night words, a journey. I am so washed
Out, yet I smile through the exhaustion.
Projection of water, a silver lust for beauty,
Darkness shuffling across the floor. I

Can give you my everything, everything.
On no page, will you find it. The furnace
Is lit with a bunch of meows, and I go on
Obeying commands other than where stress

Takes me. But I begin ruminating by lamplight,
And you, sweet creature stand exaggerated
By fluid passages. I am no more blush than
Heartache, and something of its own nature

Are the insistent lassitudes of daylight going
Down. I dreamed you once in armor, in the
Noble fiction of a summer storm. What I have,
Take it with a stir of an old dish, filled with goodness.

Small

A mere impermanent screen, a shifting
With irascible movements. Something
Needed to put this all to rest, the fictive
Overturning of those fallen into "contemplation."

A bickering, oh, how everything can be
Characterized. Even (maybe especially) me,
Who is so much smaller than this world.
Sketches lined with wood, the brow of speech

On our spectral elaborations, a girl is wearing
Silk somewhere, and somewhere I go to
Greet my destiny, clutching hard to no image.
In an overturned ship, we lay balanced on

The trees growing in the water. In a cornfield
That no one foretold, I rise to meet you.

A Triumph of Love

Beneath the unstoppable sun, we have
Grown accustomed to that which abandons
The body, beyond description or knowledge.
Without condemnation, the ridged arms

Of daylight throw themselves around us.
What church should I go to? None. I am
Just here, waiting on you to greet me from
Far beyond, and to recast yourself above

The grass. That percussive noise goes once,
Twice, the mechanics of it stay still while life
Staggers on. Scraps of paper, the glamor
Of your clear eyes, the arc of a city street,

The everything of the wind. Whose question
Is it? I am breathing on the smile of this harbor,
And I don't know where I put my shoes. I go
Toward a salved equipoise, and kiss your mercury roots.

The Freedom

One taste of freedom in the cool spring air,
And we are gathered here together, with
Linguistics and a contraption of pure joy.
I left you. I mean it. Then, I came back,

And you were all bruised. You never gave
Me a warning. The mussels pulled your teeth
That day. I am all out of compassion, but
The imperial body of water at your feet

Seemed positively various! Whatever
Happens. Whatever the wounds say in
The half-light of the stars. Ripped open,
You are only a context, a galloping nodule

Of a slow parallel. Resemblance in the
Pine trees, no scorn for wasting what is
On the table, I sing to you, I sing of you,
And a slow arriving at our detailed caesura.

On Surgery

Your ankle in phosphorescent outline,
No mention of the outlawed alphabet.
How will I "take care" of, how will I then
Block what awaits us? Home is where

The summer fog goes ballistic. I call
It endless, I call it too late for the soliloquies
That keep us. In the next hall, there
Is black and blue winter leaving us. We

Come away from this story changed, like
The letters on a bulletin board. What
Looks to be ground down, what looks like
It has been favored and then retreats

Is the cancelling out of vulgar glasses on
A nightstand filled with coffee stains. My
Friend, you were these aspects, and haloed
We can reveal the sky peeking into our chambers.

Humanity

The long-promised gold in the present
Moment, the roads of form and the
Nights are still. Where are the shipwrecked
Passages of elegy for the world? What

Unveils the drums of chrome? I am coming
To the world as it is. I am feeling the wind
Through the grass and crying. The highways
Raise their questions, the mechanical

Breathing of one so bereft. But still, I go
Through these falling cities like a spirit's
Scrawl, I carry myself against a firmament
Of life's blood like a blurred kitchen light.

I have something to offer you now, a
Question of light in bas-relief. The sheen
Of petals thinking, the endlessly permitted
Claim that we are all together in this grid.

A Century

February stars, the humid forests. I
Am routing my honesty around, the light
Is fickle here. Tonight, the shut rooms
Where we embroidered globes and ate
Moss, you cannot tell what habitation we
Will go to next. The glass resembles a
Fire, the tatterdemalion is the subject
Of the assassin. It was winter in those
Times, always. Ash Wednesday just around
The corner—what will you give up? I gave
Up almost everything, and now I stand,
Pulverized by God. The pure glee at a diamond,
Gone from me. A century passed. I lost. I won.

www.ingramcontent.com/pod-product-compliance
Lightning Source LLC
Chambersburg PA
CBHW061315040426
42444CB00010B/2649